50 Ultimate Garlic Dip Recipes

(50 Ultimate Garlic Dip Recipes - Volume 1)

Grace Wilson

Copyright: Published in the United States by Grace Wilson/ © GRACE WILSON

Published on November, 24 2020

All rights reserved. No part of this publication may be reproduced, stored in retrieval system, copied in any form or by any means, electronic, mechanical, photocopying, recording or otherwise transmitted without written permission from the publisher. Please do not participate in or encourage piracy of this material in any way. You must not circulate this book in any format. GRACE WILSON does not control or direct users' actions and is not responsible for the information or content shared, harm and/or actions of the book readers.

In accordance with the U.S. Copyright Act of 1976, the scanning, uploading and electronic sharing of any part of this book without the permission of the publisher constitute unlawful piracy and theft of the author's intellectual property. If you would like to use material from the book (other than just simply for reviewing the book), prior permission must be obtained by contacting the author at author@oreganorecipes.com

Thank you for your support of the author's rights.

Content

50 AWESOME GARLIC DIP RECIPES 4

1. A Twist On Guacamole Recipe 4
2. Amazing Garlic Hummus Recipe 4
3. Avocado Salsa Recipe 4
4. Bacon Dip Recipe 5
5. Bean Dip Recipe 5
6. Beths PicaDeGallo Recipe 5
7. Black Bean Dip In Layers Recipe 6
8. Blue Cheese Dip Recipe 6
9. Bold Beef Dip Recipe 6
10. Buffalo Chicken Dip Recipe 7
11. Bug Dip Recipe 7
12. CURRY DIP FOR CRUDITES Hawaiian Recipe Recipe 7
13. Cheddar Pretzel Dip Recipe 7
14. Cheesy Hot Crab And Red Pepper Dip Recipe 8
15. Chicken And Pistachio Pate Recipe 8
16. Chipolte Fire Sauce Recipe 9
17. Chutney Cheese Ball Recipe 9
18. Crandberry Salsa Recipe 9
19. Creamy Garlic Spinach Dip Recipe 10
20. Disney Nacho Cheese Dip Copycat Recipe Recipe 10
21. Drunkin Dip Recipe 11
22. Easy Spinach Artichoke Dip Recipe 11
23. Emerils Baked Spinach And Artichoke Dip Recipe 11
24. Emerils Fresh Tomato And Black Bean Salsa Recipe 12
25. Guacamole With Roasted Tomatillos And Tomato Recipe 12
26. Guajillo Salsa Recipe 12
27. Healthier Yogurt Cheese Dip Recipe 13
28. Herb Dip And Oil For Bread Recipe 13
29. Homemade Corn And Tomato Salsa Recipe 14
30. Hot And Spicy Spinach Dip Recipe 14
31. Hummus With Chipotle Recipe 14
32. Mexicorn Dip Recipe 15
33. My Salsa Recipe 15
34. Pico De Gallo Recipe 15
35. Radish Dip Recipe 16
36. Raw Vegan "nacho Cheese" Sauce Recipe 16
37. Roasted Red Pepper Salsa Recipe 16
38. Roasted Tomatillo Salsa Recipe 17
39. Rockin Cheesy Baked Onion Dip Recipe . 17
40. Salsa Fresca Recipe 17
41. Slammin Onion Dip Recipe 18
42. Spinach Artichoke Dip Recipe 18
43. Spinach Parmesan Dip Recipe 18
44. Sweet Potato Dip Recipe 19
45. THE Best Bean Dip EVER Recipe 19
46. Tlaquepaque Guacamole Recipe 19
47. Tuna And Egg Dip Recipe 20
48. Uniquely Devilish Veggie Dip Recipe 20
49. Universal Black Bean Salsa Recipe 20
50. White Bean Dip With Garlic Recipe 20

INDEX 22

CONCLUSION 23

50 Awesome Garlic Dip Recipes

***

1. A Twist On Guacamole Recipe

Serving: 0 | Prep: | Cook: 30mins | Ready in:

Ingredients

- 1 small white onion
- 1 clove garlic, minced
- 4 avocados
- 1/2 lime
- 1/2 teaspoon salt, or to taste
- a few big pinches of cumin powder
- a few big pinches of Indian curry powder
- dehydrated crackers

Direction

- In a small bowl combine the onion, garlic, and avocado flesh. Take the lime and give a generous squeeze or two. Add the salt, cumin and curry powder. Give everything a good stir, but don't overdo it. Taste. Now start adjusting. Do you need a bit more lime? A bit more salt? Want a stronger curry flavor? Go for it.
- Serve in a bowl with a big pile of the dehydrated crackers on the side and a sprinkling of curry powder on top (a bit of chopped cilantro would look nice as well).
- Makes one party platter.

2. Amazing Garlic Hummus Recipe

Serving: 0 | Prep: | Cook: 15mins | Ready in:

Ingredients

- 2 cans NAME BRAND garbanzo beans
- 2 Tbsp garlic paste or crushed garlic
- 8 oz Philly cream cheese
- 1 tbsp oregano/ italian seasonings
- salt to taste

Direction

- Boil your garbanzo beans about 10 minutes, until soft.
- Drain, place in bowl, mix with electric mixer. Add in the rest of the ingredients until creamy.

3. Avocado Salsa Recipe

Serving: 4 | Prep: | Cook: | Ready in:

Ingredients

- 1 (16 ounce) package frozen corn kernels, thawed
- 2 (2.25 ounce) cans sliced ripe olives, drained
- 1 red bell pepper, chopped
- 1 small onion, chopped
- 5 cloves garlic, minced
- 1/3 cup olive oil
- 1/4 cup lemon juice
- 3 tablespoons cider vinegar
- 1 teaspoon dried oregano
- 1/2 teaspoon salt
- 1/2 teaspoon ground black pepper
- 4 avocados - peeled, pitted and diced

Direction

- In a large bowl, mix corn, olives, red bell pepper and onion.

- 2. In a small bowl, mix garlic, olive oil, lemon juice, cider vinegar, oregano, salt and pepper. Pour into the corn mixture and toss to coat. Cover and chill in the refrigerator 8 hours, or overnight.
- 3. Stir avocados into the mixture before serving.

4. Bacon Dip Recipe

Serving: 12 | Prep: | Cook: | Ready in:

Ingredients

- 1 cup sour cream
- 1 2 tablespoon instant bacon bits
- 1 teaspoon instant beef bouillon
- 1 tablespoon instant minced onion
- 1/8 teaspoon minced garlic

Direction

- Combine all ingredients and mix well then refrigerate at least 2 hours before serving.

5. Bean Dip Recipe

Serving: 0 | Prep: | Cook: 1hours | Ready in:

Ingredients

- 1 15oz. can pinto beans, drained
- 4 bottled jalapeno slices (nacho slices)
- 1 tbs juice from bottled jalapeno slices
- 1/2 tsp salt
- 1/2 tsp granulated sugar
- 1/4 tsp onion powder
- 1/4 tsp paprika
- 1/8 tsp garlic powder
- 1/8 tsp cayenne pepper

Direction

- Combine drained pinto beans with the other ingredients in a food processor. Puree ingredients on high speed until smooth. Cover and chill for at least an hour before serving.

6. Beths PicaDeGallo Recipe

Serving: 8 | Prep: | Cook: | Ready in:

Ingredients

- 6-large tomatoes
- 1-lg sweet onion
- 6-10 jalapenos
- 1-bunch of cilantro
- 1/2 tsp salt
- 1/4 tsp black pepper
- 1 1/2 tsp chopped garlic (jar) i cant measure fresh. i'll mess it up. haha

Direction

- Wash all veggies
- Peel tomatoes
- Devein and deseed Jalapeños (unless u can stand the heat)
- Chop all by hand or use the Vidalia onion chopper from Wal-Mart/Walgreens also (awesome is all I can say) all my friends now own one of these. It works perfect on the small chopping even TOMATOES....
- Pour all into large bowl (tomatoes, onions, cilantro, and jalapeños)
- Add garlic
- Add salt & pepper
- Stir and taste
- Season as needed on salt or garlic.
- Love, love, love
- Serve with Tostada round chips

7. Black Bean Dip In Layers Recipe

Serving: 12 | Prep: | Cook: | Ready in:

Ingredients

- 1 15-ounce can black beans, rinsed and drained
- 1 4-ounce can chopped ripe olives, drained
- 1 small onion, finely chopped (¼ cup)
- 1 clove garlic, finely chopped
- 2 tablespoons vegetable oil
- 2 tablespoons lime juice
- ¼ teaspoon salt
- ¼ teaspoon crushed red pepper
- ¼ teaspoon ground cumin
- 1/8 teaspoon pepper
- 1 8-ounce pkg. cream cheese, softened
- 2 hard-cooked eggs, chopped
- ¼ cup finely chopped red bell pepper
- 1 medium green onion, sliced
- tortilla chips

Direction

- Mix beans, olives, chopped onion, garlic, oil, lime juice, salt, crushed red pepper, cumin and pepper.
- Cover and refrigerate 1 to 2 hours to blend flavours.
- Spread cream cheese on serving plate.
- Spoon bean mixture evenly over cream cheese
- Arrange eggs on bean mixture in ring around edge of plate.
- Sprinkle bell pepper and green onion over bean mixture.
- Serve with tortilla chips.

8. Blue Cheese Dip Recipe

Serving: 8 | Prep: | Cook: | Ready in:

Ingredients

- 1 cup mayonnaise
- 1 cup sour cream
- 4 green onions, finely chopped
- 2 tablespoons dried parsley
- 4 ounces blue cheese, crumbled
- garlic salt to taste

Direction

- 1. In a medium bowl, mix mayonnaise, sour cream, green onions, dried parsley, blue cheese and garlic salt. Cover and chill in the refrigerator until serving.

9. Bold Beef Dip Recipe

Serving: 4 | Prep: | Cook: 15mins | Ready in:

Ingredients

- 1 lb ground beef
- 1/2 cup chopped onion
- 1 clove garlic, minced
- 8 oz can tomato sauce
- 3/4 tsp oregano, crushed
- 1 tsp sugar
- 8 oz cream cheese, softened
- 1/3 cup grated parmesan cheese
- 1/4 cup catsup

Direction

- Cook ground beef, onion and garlic until beef is lightly browned and onion is tender.
- Stir in tomato sauce, catsup oregano and sugar. Cover, simmer gently for 10 minutes.
- Spoon off excess fat. Remove from heat and add cream cheese, and parmesan; stir until cream cheese has melted and is well combined.
- Serve warm with Ritz crackers or Wheat thins.
- Makes 3 cups

10. Buffalo Chicken Dip Recipe

Serving: 8 | Prep: | Cook: 20mins | Ready in:

Ingredients

- 1/2 lb chicken breasts (boneless, skinless)
- 1/2 bottle Franks Red Hot buffalo wing sauce
- 1 pkg cream cheese (softened)
- 1/2 bottle Hidden Valley Ranch dressing
- 1 C cheddar cheese
- dash Lawry's garlic salt
- Tostitos Scoops tortilla chips for dipping

Direction

- Preheat oven to 350.
- Place chicken breasts in a pot and cover with water (about an inch above the top of the chicken). Add a bit of chicken bouillon to the pot with the chicken to flavor the meat.
- While chicken is boiling, beat cream cheese and ranch together and spread into the bottom of an 8x8 or similar size pan.
- When chicken is opaque and firm to the touch (about 15-20 minutes), remove from water and let cool slightly before chopping.
- Chop chicken into small dices and add buffalo sauce and stir to coat.
- Spread chicken mixture on cheese mixture and top with cheddar cheese and sprinkle with a dash of garlic salt.
- Bake until cheese is melted.
- Serve with tortilla chips and enjoy!

11. Bug Dip Recipe

Serving: 6 | Prep: | Cook: | Ready in:

Ingredients

- 2 can of rotel diced tomatoes and green chilies, finely chopped
- 1 can black olives, finely chopped
- 2 cloves fresh garlic, finely chopped
- 1 white or yellow onion, finely chopped
- 1 tbsp vinegar
- 2 tbsp vegetable oil
- tortilla chips

Direction

- In bowl mix chopped ingredients with vinegar and oil.
- Stir well.
- Eat with tortilla chips or on tacos.
- Refrigerate before eating for better flavour.

12. CURRY DIP FOR CRUDITES Hawaiian Recipe Recipe

Serving: 8 | Prep: | Cook: | Ready in:

Ingredients

- 2 cups mayonnaise
- 1/2 cup sour cream
- 1/4 tsp turmeric
- 1 tb curry powder
- 2 garlic cloves, well minced
- 4 tsp sugar
- salt to taste
- 2 tsp fresh lemon juice
- 1/4 cup fresh minced cilantrillo

Direction

- Combine ingredients. Blend thoroughly. Chill overnight to enhance the flavour. Carrots, celery, zucchini, cherry tomatoes, large black pitted olives, mushrooms and broccoli are good to serve as crudités with this dip.

13. Cheddar Pretzel Dip Recipe

Serving: 2 | Prep: | Cook: 5mins | Ready in:

Ingredients

- 8 ounces sharp cheddar cheese, grated
- 3 cloves garlic, peeled
- 1 teaspoon salt
- 2 ounces cream cheese, softened
- 2 tablespoons unsalted butter, softened
- 1 tablespoon Dijon mustard
- 2 tablespoons yellow mustard

Direction

- Mince garlic with salt. In a bowl, combine garlic mixture and cream cheese. Mix until smooth.
- Add shredded Cheddar cheese and mix, or blend in a food processor until smooth.
- Add butter and mustards and mix again until smooth. Scrape down the sides of the bowl and mix or blend one more time.
- Serve at room temperature or slightly warmed.

14. Cheesy Hot Crab And Red Pepper Dip Recipe

Serving: 0 | Prep: | Cook: 30mins | Ready in:

Ingredients

- 1.5 cups Shredded Mozzarella
- 1 pkg (8oz) cream cheese, softened
- 1 tsp. garlic powder
- 1 tsp. italian seasoning
- 1 medium red pepper, chopped
- 1 small onion, finely chopped
- 1 can (6oz) crabmeat, drained
- Recommended one box of crackers for scooping

Direction

- PREHEAT oven to 375F.
- Remove 1/2 cup of mozzarella cheese, cover and refrigerate until ready to use.
- Mix all remaining ingredients except crackers until well blended.
- SPREAD into 9" pie plate.
- BAKE 20 minutes or until crab mixture is heated through and top is lightly browned.
- Sprinkle with reserved 1/2 cup mozzarella cheese.
- Serve hot with crackers.

15. Chicken And Pistachio Pate Recipe

Serving: 10 | Prep: | Cook: 90mins | Ready in:

Ingredients

- 2 pounds boneless chicken meat
- 1 (6-ounce) skinless boneless chicken breast
- 2/3 cup fresh white breadcrumbs
- 1/2 cup hevy cream
- 1 egg white
- 4 scallions, finely chopped
- 1 garlic clove, finely chopped
- 3 ounces cooked ham, cut in 3/8-inch cubes
- 1/2 cup shelled pistachio nuts
- 3 tablespoons chopped fresh tarragon
- pinch ground nutmeg
- 3/4 teaspoon salt
- 1 1/2 teaspoon pepper
- green salad to serve

Direction

- 1. Trim all the fat, tendons and connective tissue from the 2 pounds chicken meat and cut into 2 inch cubes. Put in a food processor fitted with a metal blade and pulse to chop the meat to a smooth puree in two or three batches. Or alternatively pass the meat through the medium or fine blade of a food mill. Remove any white stringy pieces.
- 2. Preheat the oven to 350°F. Using a sharp knife, cut the chicken breast fillet into 3/8 inch cubes.
- 3. In a large mixing bowl, soak the breadcrumbs in the cream. Add the pureed chicken, egg white, scallions, garlic, ham,

pistachio nuts, tarragon, nutmeg and salt and pepper. Using a wooden spoon or your fingers, mix until very well combined.
- 4. Lay out a piece of extra wide strong foil about 18 inches long on a work surface and lightly brush oil on a 12 inch square in the centre Spoon the chicken mixture onto the foil to form a log-shape about 12 inches long and 3 1/2 inches thick across the width of the foil. Bring together the long sides of the foil and fold over securely to enclose. Twist the ends of the foil and tie with string.
- 5. Transfer to a baking dish and bake for 1 1/2 hours. Let cool in the dish and chill until cold, preferably overnight. Serve the pate sliced with a green salad and a crusty loaf of French bread.

16. Chipolte Fire Sauce Recipe

Serving: 10 | Prep: | Cook: | Ready in:

Ingredients

- 3 cups chopped tomatoes (I prefer using Roma)
- 3/4 cup chopped fresh cilantro
- 3 tablespoons fresh lime juice
- 1/3 cup chopped onion
- 3 cloves minced garlic (optional) (I say a MUST)
- 1 or 2 seeded minced jalapeno pepper(s) (I use 3)
- 1 1/2 tbls. chopped canned chipotle chilies in adobo sauce
- 1/2 tsp. ground cumin
- salt & pepper to taste
- Sliced limes to garnish

Direction

- Combine all ingredients in medium bowl (except limes). Season with salt and pepper. Serve with sliced limes and chips of choice.
- Makes 3 cups

17. Chutney Cheese Ball Recipe

Serving: 10 | Prep: | Cook: | Ready in:

Ingredients

- 16 ounces cream cheese, softened
- ½ cup Old Farmhouse chutney (or any chutney)
- ¼ cup finely chopped scallions, white and pale green parts
- 1 medium garlic clove, minced
- ½ cup shredded colby cheese
- ½ cup shredded monterey jack cheese
- salt and freshly ground black pepper to taste
- 1 cup coarsely chopped pecans

Direction

- In medium bowl, combine cream cheese, chutney, scallions and garlic.
- Stir until well blended.
- Add Colby and Monterey Jack cheeses and stir to combine.
- Season with salt and pepper.
- Chill for several hours to firm up.
- Form into a ball and roll in the chopped pecans.
- Garnish and serve with apple wedges.

18. Crandberry Salsa Recipe

Serving: 6 | Prep: | Cook: 20mins | Ready in:

Ingredients

- 12 oz Bag cranberries
- 3/4 c sugar
- 1 garlic clove(s)-minced
- 1 (or 2) jalapeºo chilies-seeded and minced
- 1/3 c cilantro, chopped
- 3 scallions, minced

- 1/4 c lime juice
- 1 ds hot sauce
- salt and pepper

Direction

- Pick through the cranberries, removing any stems, and wash thoroughly. Bring 2 cups water and 3/4 cup sugar to a boil. Reduce the heat, add the cranberries, and simmer for 2-3 minutes, or until cooked but still firm. Do not overcook; the cranberries should keep their shape. Drain in a colander. Refresh under cold water and drain thoroughly. Mix all other ingredients with cranberry mixture and enjoy

19. Creamy Garlic Spinach Dip Recipe

Serving: 8 | Prep: | Cook: 15mins | Ready in:

Ingredients

- 2 tablespoons butter
- 2 tablespoons olive oil
- 1 3/4 cups chopped onion
- 6 large garlic cloves, minced
- 2 tablespoons all purpose flour
- 1/2 cup chicken stock or canned low-salt chicken broth
- 1/2 cup whipping cream
- 1 10-ounce package fresh spinach leaves, roughly chopped
- 1 cup (packed) grated parmesan cheese
- Handful of shredded mozzarella, to taste
- 1/4 cup sour cream
- 1/2 teaspoon cayenne pepper
- Tostito Baked Scoops -or- baguette slices, toasted

Direction

- Melt butter with oil in heavy large pot over medium heat.
- Add onion, sauté until onion is almost tender, about 5 minutes.
- Add garlic, sauté mixture another 1 - 2 minutes.
- Add flour; stir 2 minutes.
- Gradually whisk in stock and cream; bring to boil, whisking constantly.
- Cook until mixture thickens, stirring frequently, about 2 minutes.
- Remove from heat. Stir in spinach, cheeses, sour cream and cayenne (spinach will wilt).
- Season with salt and pepper.
- Transfer dip to serving bowl. Serve warm with chips or toasted baguette slices.

20. Disney Nacho Cheese Dip Copycat Recipe Recipe

Serving: 15 | Prep: | Cook: 10mins | Ready in:

Ingredients

- 1/2 pound provolone cheese, grated
- 1/2 pound American cheese, grated
- 3/4 cup heavy cream
- 8 ounces cream cheese
- 1/4 teaspoon garlic powder
- 3/4 teaspoon Worcestershire
- 1/8 teaspoon cayenne
- 1/8 teaspoon yellow food coloring

Direction

- Melt provolone in top of double boiler over boiling water.
- Add American cheese and stir in cream.
- Add cream cheese and stir until all is melted.
- Remove from heat; whip in seasonings and food colouring.
- Transfer to crockpot, and keep warm on lowest setting.
- Serve warm with crackers, chips, or veggies.

21. Drunkin Dip Recipe

Serving: 12 | Prep: | Cook: |Ready in:

Ingredients

- 1- 8 ounce package cream cheese, softened
- 1- 8 ounce package processed cheese, (ie: Velveeta) brought to room temperature
- 1/2 cup beer
- 1/2 teaspoon garlic powder, or to taste

Direction

- Mix together cream cheese and processed cheese, using an electric mixer, until completely smooth and creamy.
- Add beer and garlic powder and beat until fully incorporated and smooth.
- Refrigerate until cold.
- Serve.
- NOTE: Preparation time does not include time for chilling.

22. Easy Spinach Artichoke Dip Recipe

Serving: 10 | Prep: | Cook: 10mins |Ready in:

Ingredients

- 1 pkg. cream cheese, softened
- 1 pkg. 10 oz. frozen chopped spinach, thawed, drained
- 1 jar 7.5 oz. marinated artichoke hearts, drained, chopped
- 1 cup KRAFT Shredded mozzarella cheese
- 1/2 tsp. minced garlic
- 1/4 cup parmesan cheese

Direction

- Spread cream cheese onto bottom of pie plate.
- Mix spinach, artichokes, mozzarella cheese and until well blended; spread over cream cheese. Sprinkle with Parmesan cheese.
- Microwave on HIGH 3 min. or until heated through.

23. Emerils Baked Spinach And Artichoke Dip Recipe

Serving: 10 | Prep: | Cook: 15mins |Ready in:

Ingredients

- 1/4 cup plus 2 tablespoons vegetable oil
- 1/4 cup all-purpose flour
- 2 cups milk
- salt
- cayenne pepper
- 1/2 cup grated Parmesan (about 2 ounces)
- 1/2 cup grated Monterey Jack (about 2 ounces)
- 1 cup chopped onions
- 1 (10-ounce) bag fresh spinach, stemmed, rinsed and chopped
- 2 tablespoons chopped garlic
- 2 (15-ounce) cans artichoke hearts, drained and julienned

Direction

- Preheat the oven to 400 degrees F.
- Combine 1/4 cup of the vegetable oil and flour in a saucepan over medium heat. Stir the mixture constantly 5 to 6 minutes for a blond roux.
- Whisk in the milk and bring the liquid up to a boil.
- Season the liquid with salt and cayenne.
- Simmer the liquid for 5 to 6 minutes, or until the liquid is thick and coats the back of a spoon.
- Remove the sauce from the heat and stir in the cheeses. Set the sauce aside.
- In a sauté pan, heat the remaining 2 tablespoons vegetable oil. When the oil is hot, add the onions and sauté for 2 minutes.
- Stir in handfuls of spinach at a time, until all the spinach is incorporated. Add the garlic and

- artichoke and sauté for 2 minutes. Season the vegetables with salt and cayenne.
- Remove the vegetables from the heat and turn into a mixing bowl. Fold the cheese sauce into the vegetables.
- Turn the mixture into a baking pan. Bake the dip for 10 to 15 minutes, or until the top is golden brown.

24. Emerils Fresh Tomato And Black Bean Salsa Recipe

Serving: 12 | Prep: | Cook: 1mins | Ready in:

Ingredients

- 4 cups chopped vine-ripened tomatoes
- 2 cups dried black beans, cooked in salted water until tender, cooled (about 2 cups)
- 1 cup small diced red onions
- 1 large fresh jalapeno, seed and cut into small dice
- 1/2 cup loosely packed chopped fresh cilantro leaves
- 1 tablespoon chopped fresh parsley leaves
- 1 tablespoon chopped garlic
- Salt
- Freshly ground black pepper
- 6 tablespoons fresh lime juice
- 1 tablespoon extra-virgin olive oil
- Crispy corn tortilla chips

Direction

- Combine the first seven ingredients in a mixing bowl.
- Season with salt and pepper.
- Add the lime juice and olive oil.
- Mix well.
- Spoon into a serving bowl and serve with the chips.

25. Guacamole With Roasted Tomatillos And Tomato Recipe

Serving: 5 | Prep: | Cook: 30mins | Ready in:

Ingredients

- 2-3 avocados
- 1 medium tomato
- 4-6 tomatillos
- 1 clove of garlic
- 1 Tablespoon lime juice
- 1 small-medium onion
- 1/2 cup chopped fresh cilantro
- 1 or 2 jalapeno peppers
- salt and pepper to taste

Direction

- Roast the tomatillos and tomato on the grill. You may want to place them on a sheet of foil (to reduce mess). Grill on each side until they become darkened (about 5-10 min). Gently remove from heat and set aside to cool.
- Mince onion, garlic, cilantro and jalapeno and add to a bowl.
- Add lime juice.
- Peel and pit avocados and mash avocados in bowl with the other ingredients.
- Chop/mash the roasted tomatillos and tomato and add to bowl and mix everything up into a paste.
- Salt and pepper to taste.
- Serve alongside chips or fresh veggies.

26. Guajillo Salsa Recipe

Serving: 3 | Prep: | Cook: 5mins | Ready in:

Ingredients

- 1/2 lb dried Guajillo Chiles (Dried NuMex Chiles will work)
- 3 cups water
- 6 large cloves roasted garlic

- 1 1/2 Tsp toasted and ground cumin Seeds
- 1 Tsp salt
- 1/2 lb roma tomatoes peeled and seeded
- 2 Tsp toasted pumpkin seeds
- 1/3 cup apple Cidar vinegar
- 1 Tsp toasted and ground Mexican oregano

Direction

- Remove stems from Chiles. Heat a heavy skillet on medium heat. Throw in dried Chiles and dry toast 3 - 4 minutes shaking the pan to prevent them from burning. They should become quite aromatic and the skin should feel hot and begin to soften a little.
- In a med - large saucepan bring the 3 Cups of water to a boil. Place Toasted Chiles in boiling water. Boil for 1 minute, cover and let sit for about 20 minutes until Chiles are soft and rehydrated.
- In a blender, puree the Chiles with the remaining ingredients. Chill for at least 30 mins. Serve Cold with Tortilla chips.
- To serve as a sauce: Heat 2 Tbsp. Peanut Oil in a high sided pan and refry the sauce at a sizzle for 3 - 5 mins. Add a little water if it gets too thick.
- I have used this sauce to baste Shrimp and Scallop Kabobs or spoon a small pool on a plate and place grilled kabobs on top of the sauce.

27. Healthier Yogurt Cheese Dip Recipe

Serving: 8 | Prep: | Cook: | Ready in:

Ingredients

- •4 tablespoons whipped cream cheese or reduced-fat cream cheese
- •10 ounces 2% Fage Greek yogurt
- •2 tablespoons parmesan cheese
- •2 teaspoons dried chives
- •3 cloves garlic, minced
- •1 tablespoon chopped onion
- Serve with crisp, lowfat crackers or crudite

Direction

- Combine all ingredients and blend well with a spoon.
- .Refrigerate for 12 hours or overnight, allowing flavours to marry. Serve with crudité or crisp, low-fat crackers.

28. Herb Dip And Oil For Bread Recipe

Serving: 6 | Prep: | Cook: | Ready in:

Ingredients

- These are all approximate...Use more or less based on your taste. I used fresh herbs (because I had them), but I'm sure dried herbs would be just as delicious!
- All herbs should be finely chopped.
- 1/2 teaspoon crushed red pepper
- 1/2 teaspoon ground black pepper
- 1 teaspoon oregano,
- 1 teaspoon rosemary
- 1 teaspoon basil (I used lemon basil...made it extra tangy!)
- 1 teaspoon parsley
- 1 teaspoon garlic powder
- 1 teaspoon minced fresh garlic
- 1/2 teaspoon salt (I think the restaurant used more)
- 1/4 cup extra virgin olive oil (or as needed)
- bread for dipping

Direction

- Combine all ingredients EXCEPT oil, into a bowl.
- Mix together till it looks nicely blended.
- To serve, scoop whatever amount you'd like onto a dipping dish or plate.

- Pour your desired amount of olive oil over the top of this mixture.
- Dip your bread.
- Eat.
- Enjoy!
- I used individual bread dipping dishes so that everyone could use as much or as little of the dip and oil as they wanted...and double dip with no fear of embarrassment!

29. Homemade Corn And Tomato Salsa Recipe

Serving: 30 | Prep: | Cook: 60mins | Ready in:

Ingredients

- 2 gallons tomatoes peeled and chopped
- 5 pounds peeled and chopped sweet onions
- 2 pounds chopped green bell pepper
- 3 tablespoons salt
- 1 cup sugar
- 1 cup vinegar
- 2 tablespoons garlic
- 1 gallon silver queen corn cut off cobs
- 1/2 cup hot sauce

Direction

- Combine tomatoes, onions, bell pepper, salt, sugar, vinegar, garlic, corn and hot sauce.
- Cook all ingredients for 1 hour stirring often.
- When a red acid rises to the top skim off bubbles and discard.
- Cool completely before serving.

30. Hot And Spicy Spinach Dip Recipe

Serving: 12 | Prep: | Cook: 15mins | Ready in:

Ingredients

- 2 (10 ounce) boxes frozen chopped spinach
- 3 tablespoons butter
- 2 tablespoons all-purpose flour
- 1/2 cup half and half
- 1/2 cup spinach cooking liquid
- 6 ounces pepper Jack cheese, shredded
- 1/2 teaspoon ground black pepper
- 1/2 teaspoon celery salt
- 1/2 teaspoon garlic powder, or to taste
- 1 teaspoon worcestershire sauce
- tortilla chips

Direction

- Cook spinach according to package directions.
- Drain spinach well, reserving 1/2 cup cooking liquid.
- In saucepan, melt butter.
- Add flour and cook until bubbly.
- Add half and half and spinach cooking liquid.
- Cook, stirring, until mixture thickens.
- Add cheese, pepper, celery salt, garlic powder and Worcestershire.
- Fold in spinach.
- Spoon into greased 1 quart baking dish.
- Bake at 350 degrees for 15 minutes or until bubbly.
- Serve with tortilla chips.

31. Hummus With Chipotle Recipe

Serving: 6 | Prep: | Cook: | Ready in:

Ingredients

- 1 can garbanzo beans
- 3 tbls. tahini
- 1 1/2 tsp. garlic, chopped
- 1 tbls. plus 1 tsp. lemon juice
- 1 tbls. plus 1 tsp lime juice
- 2 1/2 tsp. chipotle in adobo sauce, canned and chopped
- 1 tsp. salt
- 1 tbls. cilantro, chopped (I use parsley because I don't like the taste of cilantro)

- 1/2 cup plus 2 tbls. olive oil
- salt and pepper to taste

Direction

- Put beans in processor and puree
- Add tahini, garlic, lemon juice, lime juice, chipotles, salt, and cilantro on low, mix ingredients well while adding oil in a slow, steady stream
- Season with salt and pepper

32. Mexicorn Dip Recipe

Serving: 15 | Prep: | Cook: 120mins | Ready in:

Ingredients

- 3 (11 oz) cans of mexicorn, drained
- 1/2 cup of chopped green onions
- 1 (7 oz.) can of chopped green chilies
- 1 cup of mayonnaise
- 1 cup of sour cream
- 1 lb of grated cheddar cheese
- 1 tsp pepper
- 6 oz chopped jalapeno peppers
- 1/2 tsp garlic powder

Direction

- Mix all ingredients together.
- Chill 2-3 hrs.

33. My Salsa Recipe

Serving: 8 | Prep: | Cook: 15mins | Ready in:

Ingredients

- 4 medium tomatoes (peeled and seeded)
- 1 jalapeno (seeded and diced fine)
- 1 habanero (seeded ribs removed and minced very fine)
- 1 rib celery (diced)
- 1 large onion (diced)
- 3 cloves garlic (minced)
- 1/2 green bell pepper (diced)
- 1/2 red bell pepper (diced)
- juice of 1/2 a lime
- 1/4 cup extra virgin olive oil
- 1/2 tsp. coriander
- 1/4 tsp. cinnamon
- 1/4 tsp. chili powder
- salt & pepper

Direction

- Sweat peppers, onion, and garlic over medium low heat (until translucent)
- Add salt, pepper, and spices
- Remove from heat and stir in tomatoes
- Finish with lime juice and olive oil
- Serve with chips or use as a garnish on your favourite Mexican recipe
- *for a spicier salsa do not remove seeds and ribs from the chilies
- **a few tablespoons fresh chopped cilantro can be added at the end for a brighter flavour

34. Pico De Gallo Recipe

Serving: 4 | Prep: | Cook: 1hours | Ready in:

Ingredients

- 4-5 roma tomatoes - diced
- 1 white onion - diced
- 2 jalapenos - seeded and diced
- 1/2 cup chopped fresh cilantro
- 2 garlic cloves - minced
- juice of 2 limes
- 1/4 teaspoon cumin
- 1/2 teaspoon Mexican oregano
- 1/4 teaspoon white pepper
- pinch of coriander
- 1/2 teaspoon salt (or more to taste)

Direction

- In bowl combine all ingredients and mix well. Refrigerate for about 1 hour to let flavours come together.

35. Radish Dip Recipe

Serving: 10 | Prep: | Cook: 240mins | Ready in:

Ingredients

- 1 cup finely chopped radishes
- 1 8 oz. pkg. cream cheese, room temperature
- 1 clove garlic, minced
- 1 tbls. lemon juice
- 1/2 tsp. salt
- 1/2 tsp. dried dill
- black pepper to taste

Direction

- Cook time is chill time
- Combine all ingredients and chill for 4 hours

36. Raw Vegan "nacho Cheese" Sauce Recipe

Serving: 0 | Prep: | Cook: 20mins | Ready in:

Ingredients

- 1 large red bell pepper
- 1/4 cup water
- 1 cup raw cashews (soaked over night and rinsed well)
- 1 Tablespoon tahini
- 3 Tablespoons nutritional yeast
- 1 T Raw onion
- 1 clove garlic
- 2 Tablespoons fresh lemon juice
- 1 1/2 Teaspoons salt (I use much less salt)
- For a little flavor variety, try adding:
- green onion (optional)
- jalapeno pepper (optional)
- green chilis (optional)
- red pepper flakes (optional), etc.

Direction

- Put all ingredients in the blender and blend until creamy.

37. Roasted Red Pepper Salsa Recipe

Serving: 0 | Prep: | Cook: 12mins | Ready in:

Ingredients

- 4 red bell peppers
- 1 tablespoon olive oil
- 1/2 cup dried tomatoes*
- 3 tablespoons chopped fresh basil
- 1 tablespoon balsamic vnegar
- 2 to 3 garlic cloves, minced
- 1/2 teaspoon salt
- 1/2 teaspoon fresh rosemary, finely chopped
- 1/4 teaspoon ground red pepper

Direction

- Bake peppers on an aluminum foil lined baking sheet at 500 degrees for 12 minutes or until peppers look blistered, turning once.
- Place peppers in a heavy duty zip top plastic bag seal and let stand 10 minutes to loosen skins.
- Peel peppers; remove and discard seeds.
- Coarsely chop peppers; drizzle with 1 tablespoon olive oil; set aside.
- Pour boiling water to cover over dried tomatoes. Let stand 3 minutes; drain and coarsely chop.
- Stir together bell pepper, tomato, basil, and remaining ingredients.
- Cover and chill salsa up to 2 days.
- Yield: 2 cups

- * 1/3 cup dried tomatoes in oil may be substituted for dried tomatoes; Drain tomatoes well, pressing between layers of paper towels.

38. Roasted Tomatillo Salsa Recipe

Serving: 6 | Prep: | Cook: 15mins | Ready in:

Ingredients

- 1 pound fresh tomatillos, husks discarded
- 3 cloves garlic, unpeeled
- 2 large jalapeno peppers
- 1 yellow onion, quartered
- juice of 1 lime
- 1/2 cup chopped fresh cilantro
- 2 tablespoons olive oil
- 1/2 teaspoon each: sugar, salt, freshly ground pepper

Direction

- Heat oven to 500 degrees. Place tomatillos, garlic, jalapenos and onion in an ungreased baking pan. Cook, stirring once, until vegetables are charred, about 15 minutes; set aside to cool. Remove stems (but not seeds) from peppers: discard. Peel garlic.
- Transfer ingredients to a food processor: process until coarsely chopped. Transfer to a medium bowl; stir in lime juice, cilantro, olive oil, sugar, salt and pepper until well-blended. Salsa will keep, refrigerated, up to 4 days.

39. Rockin Cheesy Baked Onion Dip Recipe

Serving: 16 | Prep: | Cook: 55mins | Ready in:

Ingredients

- 2 (8-ounce) packages cream cheese
- 1 cup regular or low-fat mayonnaise
- 1 1/2 cups grated parmesan cheese
- 1 tablespoon white wine worcestershire sauce
- 1 teaspoon Tabasco
- 1 teaspoon garlic powder
- 1 1/2 cups chopped onions (fresh or frozen; thaw and squeeze out excess liquid)
- 1 tablespoon chopped chives or green onions

Direction

- Preheat oven to 350 degrees.
- In a large bowl, combine the cream cheese, mayonnaise, Parmesan cheese, Worcestershire, Tabasco, garlic powder and chopped onions until well-combined.
- Pour into a 2- or 3-quart casserole dish.
- Sprinkle with the chives and press lightly so they adhere to the mixture.
- Bake 50 to 55 minutes, until the middle is set.
- Serve warm with crackers and chips.

40. Salsa Fresca Recipe

Serving: 8 | Prep: | Cook: | Ready in:

Ingredients

- 2 Large fresh vine ripe tomatoes, chopped
- 1/2 large white onion, peeled and minced
- 1/4 - 1/2 tsp minced fresh garlic (or more to taste)
- 1 jalapeno or habanero pepper (depends on the heat you want) stemmed, seeded, and minced.
- 1/4 cup chopped cilantro leaves
- 1 Tbsp fresh lime juice
- salt and fresh ground pepper to taste

Direction

- Combine all ingredients, taste and adjust seasoning as necessary
- Let flavours marry for 15 minutes
- Serve within 1 hour

41. Slammin Onion Dip Recipe

Serving: 20 | Prep: | Cook: | Ready in:

Ingredients

- 10 oz Dried Chopped onion
- 8 oz cream cheese, softened
- 8 oz sour cream
- White (Dry) cooking wine
- salt, pepper, dash of garlic powder
- Garnish

Direction

- In an airtight container, pour dried onion and enough white wine to completely cover.
- Seal and refrigerate overnight or until the onion has completely absorbed the wine. Usually within 2-4 hours.
- Uncover, then mix.
- Add the softened cream cheese, sour cream and mix well.
- Put salt, pepper and dash of garlic to taste. (Garlic brings out the taste of onion and visa-versa)
- Garnish with sprig of parsley or rosemary.
- *Tip: If it gets too stiff in the fridge, add a dash of white wine and beat it back to smoothness.
- Serve with bite sized veggies. I.e. Baby carrots, celery sticks, cauliflower, mushrooms, green or wax beans, etc. Try to use assorted colors for eye appeal.

42. Spinach Artichoke Dip Recipe

Serving: 10 | Prep: | Cook: 30mins | Ready in:

Ingredients

- * 2 (14 ounce) can artichoke hearts, drained and chopped
- * 1 (10 ounce) package frozen chopped spinach, thawed (all water squeezed out very important)
- * 1 cup mozzarella cheese shredded
- * 1/2 cup mayonnaise
- * 1 8 oz. brick cream cheese
- * 1 cup grated Romano, Parmesan, asiago cheeses
- * 1 teaspoon basil
- * 1/2 teaspoon minced garlic (or more to taste)
- * salt and pepper to taste

Direction

- 1. Preheat oven to 375 degrees F.
- 2. In a food processor, mix together artichoke hearts, spinach, mayonnaise, cream cheese, all the cheeses, basil and garlic. (This can be done by hand too if you want. I normally just do the spinach and artichokes in the food processor and the rest with my stand mixer).
- 3. Pour mixture into baking dish, sprayed with Pam.
- 4. Bake until heated through and bubbly, about 30 minutes.

43. Spinach Parmesan Dip Recipe

Serving: 2 | Prep: | Cook: 10mins | Ready in:

Ingredients

- 1 tsp olive oil
- 3 garlic cloves
- 1/4 tsp salt
- 10 oz's spinach
- 1/2 cup basil leaves (loosely packed)
- 1/3 cup softened cream cheese
- 1/8 tsp black pepper
- 1/3 cup fat free yogurt (plain)
- 1/4 cup parmesan cheese (grated)
- 1 lime

Direction

- Heat olive oil in a large skillet over medium-high heat. Chop garlic cloves and add the sauté for about 1 minute. Add salt and spinach and sauté for about 3 minutes or until spinach wilts. Place spinach mixture in a colander, pressing until mixture is barely moist.
- Place spinach mixture, basil, cream cheese, and pepper in a food processor; process until smooth. Spoon mixture into a decent sized bowl. Cut lime in half then squeeze the juice from the lime into the mixture and add yogurt and parmesan cheese. Stir the mixture, and then chill.

44. Sweet Potato Dip Recipe

Serving: 4 | Prep: | Cook: 90mins | Ready in:

Ingredients

- 6 small-medium sweet potatoes (about 2¼ lbs.)
- 2 tbsp. olive oil
- 4 scallions, chopped fine
- ½ cup chopped drained bottled roasted red peppers
- 1/3 cup packed fresh cilantro sprigs, washed well, dried and chopped fine
- 2 ripe tomatoes, seeded and chopped fine
- 1 large garlic clove, minced and mashed to a paste with ¼ tsp. salt
- 2 tbsp. balsamic vinegar
- ½ tsp. salt, or to taste
- ½ tsp. freshly ground black pepper, or to taste
- ½ fresh jalapeno chili, seeded and chopped fine
- ¼ - ½ cup water if necessary

Direction

- Preheat oven to 400 degrees.
- Prick potatoes with a fork and on a foil-lined baking sheet bake in the middle of the oven for 1½ hours, or until very soft.
- Cool potatoes slightly and scoop flesh into a bowl.
- In a food processor, puree potatoes with remaining ingredients,
- Adding enough water to reach desired consistency.
- Serve dip with baked or whole-grain tortilla chips or vegetable dippers.
- Makes about 4 cups.

45. THE Best Bean Dip EVER Recipe

Serving: 4 | Prep: | Cook: 60mins | Ready in:

Ingredients

- 1 (15 ounce) can pinto beans, drained and rinsed
- 4 bottled jalapeno slices
- 1 tbls. juice from bottled jalapeno slices
- 1/2 tsp. salt
- 1/2 tsp. sugar
- 1/4 tsp. onion powder
- 1/4 tsp. paprika
- 1/8 tsp. garlic powder
- 1/8 tsp. cayenne pepper

Direction

- Put all ingredients into food processor
- Puree on high until smooth
- Chill for a bit before serving
- Cook time is chill time

46. Tlaquepaque Guacamole Recipe

Serving: 12 | Prep: | Cook: | Ready in:

Ingredients

- 10 avocados, skinned and pitted
- 1 bunch cilantro, chopped fine
- 1 tomato, diced

- 1 Tbsp garlic salt
- 1/2 c lime juice
- 1 c green onion, chopped

Direction

- Smash the avocado smooth by adding the lime juice while using a potato masher.
- Mix in garlic salt, green onion, and cilantro.
- Fold in diced tomatoes.

47. Tuna And Egg Dip Recipe

Serving: 2 | Prep: | Cook: | Ready in:

Ingredients

- dash tabasco
- garlic salt to taste
- a little mayonnaise
- 1 tsp anchovy paste
- dash cayenne pepper
- 1 tsp finely minced onion
- 3 hard boiled eggs mashed
- 1/2 small can tuna drained and flaked

Direction

- In a large bowl combine the eggs, anchovy paste, tuna, onion, garlic salt, cayenne pepper, tabasco and enough mayonnaise to make a dip consistency. The Tuna and Egg Dip is really great served with crackers, cabana and cheese.

48. Uniquely Devilish Veggie Dip Recipe

Serving: 0 | Prep: | Cook: | Ready in:

Ingredients

- 1 large container of sour cream
- 1 large package of cream cheese
- 1 large can of devilled ham
- ½ package of Lipton Onion Soup Mix
- garlic salt or freshly minced garlic and salt to taste
- tobasco sauce – a couple of dashes

Direction

- Mix well and refrigerate until ready to serve.
- Serve with raw crudités…carrots, celery, jicama, green onions etc.

49. Universal Black Bean Salsa Recipe

Serving: 10 | Prep: | Cook: | Ready in:

Ingredients

- 1 bunch cilantro, finely chopped
- 6 green onions, sliced
- 1 red onion, diced
- 2 cans black beans, rinsed and drained
- 1 can diced tomatos (or 3 fresh chopped in season)
- 1-10 oz bag frozen white corn
- 3 avocadoes, diced (leave 1 pit in dish to keep from turning brown)
- 3 cloves garlic, chopped

Direction

- Mix together
- Refrigerate overnight to let flavours blend
- Enjoy!!

50. White Bean Dip With Garlic Recipe

Serving: 8 | Prep: | Cook: | Ready in:

Ingredients

- 2 cans small white beans
- 5 garlic cloves peeled
- 2 tablespoons freshly squeezed lemon juice
- 5 tablespoons extra virgin olive oil
- 1/2 teaspoon salt
- 1 teaspoon freshly ground black pepper
- 1 roma tomato seeded and diced
- 2 large bags pita bread chips

Direction

- Rinse beans under cold running water in a colander and allow to drain.
- Place garlic cloves in food processor fitted with metal blade and mince.
- Add beans and process to purée.
- Add juice, olive oil, salt and pepper then purée until mixture forms good consistency for dipping.
- Place in a serving bowl and garnish with diced tomato then accompany with pita bread chips.

Index

A
Artichoke 3,11,18
Avocado 3,4

B
Bacon 3,5
Beef 3,6
Bread 3,13

C
Carrot 7
Cheddar 3,7,8
Cheese 3,6,9,10,13,16
Chicken 3,7,8
Chipotle 3,14
Chutney 3,9
Crab 3,8
Cream 3,10

D
Dijon mustard 8

E
Egg 3,20

G
Garlic 1,3,4,10,18,20
Guacamole 3,4,12,19

H
Hummus 3,4,14

M
Mince 8,12
Mozzarella 8

O
Oil 3,13
Onion 3,17,18,20

P
Parmesan 3,11,17,18
Peel 5,12,16,17
Pepper 3,8,16
Pistachio 3,8
Potato 3,19

R
Radish 3,16

S
Salsa 3,4,9,12,14,15,16,17,20
Salt 12
Scallop 13
Seeds 13
Soup 20
Spinach 3,10,11,14,18

T
Tabasco 17
Tea 16
Tomatillo 3,12,17
Tomato 3,12,14

V
Vegan 3,16

Conclusion

Thank you again for downloading this book!

I hope you enjoyed reading about my book!

If you enjoyed this book, please take the time to share your thoughts and post a review on Amazon. It'd be greatly appreciated!

Write me an honest review about the book – I truly value your opinion and thoughts and I will incorporate them into my next book, which is already underway.

Thank you!

If you have any questions, **feel free to contact at:** *author@oreganorecipes.com*

Grace Wilson

oreganorecipes.com

Your Note

Your Note

Your Note

Your Note

Your Note

Printed in Great Britain
by Amazon